STRINGS OF MY HEART

A poetic exploration of Love,
Heartache, Faith and Inspiration

S S SAWANT

BookLeaf Publishing

India | USA | UK

Made with ♥ on the BookLeaf Publishing Platform
www.bookleafpub.in
www.bookleafpub.com

Dedicated to my late father, Mr Sudhir Namdeo Sawant.

May your legacy of reading and writing be remembered and carried forward.

Acknowledgement

I could have never completed this wonderful expedition of art without these incredible people:

Mrs. Sujata Sudhir Sawant - My lovely mother, whose constant encouragement has always nurtured the artist in me.

Mr. Sunil Sudhir Sawant - My beloved brother, for always supporting me and believing in my actions.

Mrs Sampada Sunil Sawant - My dear sister-in-law, for always having faith in my dreams.

Dr. Madhura Sharad Nikam - Without you, this wouldn't have been possible.

Mrs Jyoti Dayashankar Pandey - My teacher, whose insightful guidance and sharp intellect have enriched my work.

I am deeply grateful to each of you.

Preface

The rich and evocative language of the poetic realm is something the heart instinctively yearns for. Weaving words together and making them dance between the lines ends up in an art soothing to the mind. Words are powerful, persuasive, and convincing which will take you on a roller coaster full of love, thrill and motivation. Words also express your sorrow and heartbreak. Words motivate you, inspire you and help you endure.

Over time, I have forged a profound friendship with words. I must admit, they have proved their friendship and have never broken my trust. They remain with me, within me... always... flowing through my veins. I cherish them, much like an artisan shaping raw material into a masterpiece. I have been writing a lot since a considerable period of time. But this piece of artwork has become my first published artistry. It'll take you to the depths of your heart, allowing you to feel love through the lines. It'll rekindle your charismatic smile, instill a sense of hope, and empower you to bounce back from the adversities of life. It'll help you connect with the pain, fall in love again, revisit devastating heartbreaks, and inspire for the amazing life ahead.

Strings of My Heart is a melody flowing straight from my soul to yours. It is a poetic exploration of love, heartache, faith and inspiration.

THE SUN IS RISING

Gone are the days of boring nights and weary
daylights,
Welcome the journey, with some useless
fights.
The warmth of your gaze and the calm of my
embrace,
When intertwined, will dance in love's grace
Dive into a world where we together will take
free flight...
The sun is rising, to bathe us in light...

Forget the sorrows, pack some excitement,
Hold my hand, let's march towards the best of
our amusements.
The beauty of your smile and the mesmerized
heartbeats of mine,

When intertwined, will age like fine wine.
To hear you talk unstoppably and make me go
numb and quiet,
The sun is rising, to make us shine bright.

Behold the breath, adventures call our name,
Best or worst? Who cares? When we both ride
the same flame!
The child in your heart and child in my mind,
When intertwined, will spring the toddler
hard to find.
To make you jump merrily and make me
laugh the heart out,
The sun is rising, to make our lives beautifully
sprout.

Now, don't go down the river, tears don't
exist anymore,
Let's feel the thrill of this relation, deep down
in the core.
The tip of your saree and the sacred cloth on
my shoulder,
When intertwined, will make us
wonder....and wonder...

To give us the new beginning and hold us in
embrace forever tight.
Look out the window!!!
The sun has already risen, to make us feel the
light!

Twinkling Lady, Scorching Sun

Under the shield of the moonlit night,
My eyes search for the rhythm of life.
What if a lassie descends, jolting the boredom
in my veins?
Igniting a fire in my forsaken heart, with her
beauty and brain?

Shining through the darkness, a glittering star
winked at me...
Dumbfounded bones of mine, shivered as the
star jumped into the abyssal sea.
The lassie I dreamt of walked out of the water,
shining like the star I saw...

Her mesmerising elegance made me lose grip
on the jaw...
Since I was unable to hold back exciting
delirium,
I let her dissolve into my flesh and bones.
The splendid vigour of that twinkling lady,
glinted from my head to toe, hypnotised I
grinned, as she penetrated her glimmering
flones.

Under the wrap of darker night,
The eyes are searching the pieces of light...
What if I had never dreamt of the lassie,
liberating the freedom in my vein?
Gasping above the rubble of my blazing
heart, I cursed—why had not I used the brain?

Shining through the darkness, the scorching
sun laughed at me,
Gobsmacked eyes of mine saw it go up above
the sea.
Tearing the shrouds around my gaze, it
illuminated infinite waters,
His confident grace made me jump in, leaving
aside my horrors.

I popped out of the water and at the helpful sun I gazed,
Awestruck, I beamed, as I found myself smiling back - confident, sanguine and blessed!!!

BECAUSE NEVER HAD I

Because never had I felt like this,
A tremor surged through my heart...
Seeing you for the first time,
I wished for something alluring to start...
Peering into your luminous eyes, I urged you
to be my dove...
From then on, Oh Baby! I started bopping to
the rhythm of love!!

Because never had I touched anyone,
A thrill cascaded down my spine...
Touching you for the first time,

I longed to make you all mine...
Brushing against your rosy skin, I proposed
you to be my dove...
Brushing on your cute cheeks, Oh Dear! I
started bopping on the rhythm of love!!

Because never had I kissed anyone,
Passion sparkled through my spirit...
Pecking you for the first time,
I fancied to forget my limit.
Pressing your soft lips, I considered you had
become my dove.
Closing my eyes amidst, Oh Sweetheart! I
started bopping to the rhythm of love!!

Because never had I loved anyone,
Adoration radiated through my eyes.
Endearing myself for the first time,
I desired to hold you, until away the time
flies.
Drowning in the depth of your warmth, you
turned me in your dove...
Transmuting from amort to amorist, Oh
Darling! I would die to this rhythm of love!!

The Goddess

Eyes... expressive and sparkling,
Beholding a yard full of flowers,
Luring me into the dreamy land,
To rejoice under aromatic shower.

Lips... moist and luscious,
Making the world falter as she smiles,
Pausing the blink of my eye,
Freezing my legs and driving me immobile.

Voice... soothing and melodic,
Turning the air soulful,
Settling the chaos in my head,
having me turned peaceful.

She... stunning and ravishing,
Crafted by grace like a fine art,
Heavenly goddess on the earth,
Has set the fire in my Heart...!

COME, BE MY VALENTINE

Come, let's waltz upon the moon,
Be passionate and whirl on the croon.
Embracing the imperfectness, let's hold
ourselves tight,
Let's choose each other above all our silly
fights.
With vows for the lifetime, brighten my life
Oh! my sunshine!
Gift me your promises, come be my
Valentine!

Rise, let's soar above the clouds,
For making our love a triumph, let's raise a
toast, standing proud.
Fathoming your irritations, I'll let you be real
and raw,
Empathizing with your thoughts, a sketch of
true love I'll draw
With the grip of your compassion, carry my
heart Oh! My lifeline!
Hand me out your art of understanding,
come be my Valentine!

Rise up, let's take a leap high beyond the blue,
Igniting the most sacred feeling, how crazy
have you made me, you have no clue.
Pinning your faith on me, you've made a bold
move,
Sprouting life out of your faith, how much I
adore you I'll prove.
Tie the knot of your trust and age with me
like a fine wine,
Devoting your soul forever, come be my
Valentine!

Wake up, fantasies no longer hide under the
eyelid,
Diving deep in the ocean of compassion, in
our own wonderland let us skid.
Your tender gaze and amorous touch, have
stirred up the life in my core,
On this journey called life, let's together
wonderfully soar,
Being smitten with me, feel deep affection in
my arms,
Standing always by my side, sharpen the
gleam of my charm.
My honey pie! Come, be all mine...!
Loving me unconditionally, come, make me
your Valentine!

Yeah! My Lady...

Yeah! My lady is like an Aspen,
Sensitive, patient, and serene,
A tranquil force on the ground,
With the ingenuity of a queen.

Yeah! My lady is like Bird of Paradise,
Joyous, cheery, and jaunty,
Compelling spirit on the earth,
Pulling me in, with her gravity

Yeah! My lady is like a Flamingo,
Fascinating, appealing, and slender,
Enticing beauty on the planet,
Driving me wild with her splendour.

Yeah! My lady is like Queen Unicorn,
Pure, magical, and rare,
The exquisite señora of my universe,
Spreading love in the air!

The Winking Night

I inhaled the briny fragrance,
Which left my innards refreshed.
Sitting on the banks of the brisk ocean that
night,
I gaped at the sky - beautifully dressed!
Amidst the distinct chatter of crickets, my
spirit pulsed with glee,
Blanketing a million stars, the night was
winking at me...!!

The sea breeze
Traced my thoughts down memory's lane.
How far have I marched in this world of crazy
creatures,
Trying to turn me insane?
The salty air kissed my face, setting my
chaotic mind free

Gifting serenity deep within the heart, the
night was winking at me...!!

As time drifted ahead,
I yearned for Kala to freeze this silent hour.
Breathing through the calmness,
I felt like a night-blooming flower,
Susurration of waves vibrated the bed of
infinite sea,
Sending the stillness through my soul, the
night was winking at me...!!

Why did I feel so sad,
When the light broke through the dark?
Back to the busy life,
It signalled me to embark.
Anticipation of meeting the ocean again let
my spirit flee,
And in the hours of darkness when I came
back,
I found the night winking at me!!

Inside The Flesh and Bones

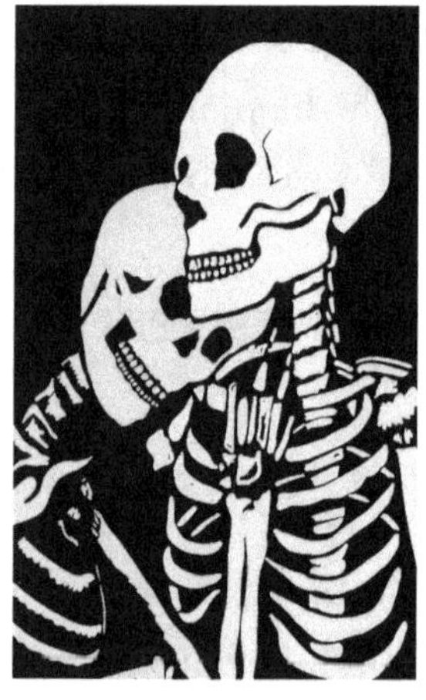

Inside the flesh and bones, who you are?

You are an inevitable soul behind that painful scar...
Which resonates through your heart, and raises your mental bar...

You are the brazen fire, which blazes to
mould you into a Czar...
You are the intrepid ice, which chills the
spine down the Jaguar...

You are the divine incarnation, boosting
yourself jump above the star,
You are the deadly Lucifer, who dances on the
chest of your own generous avatar...

Inside the flesh and bones, do you truly know
who you are?

The Mirror

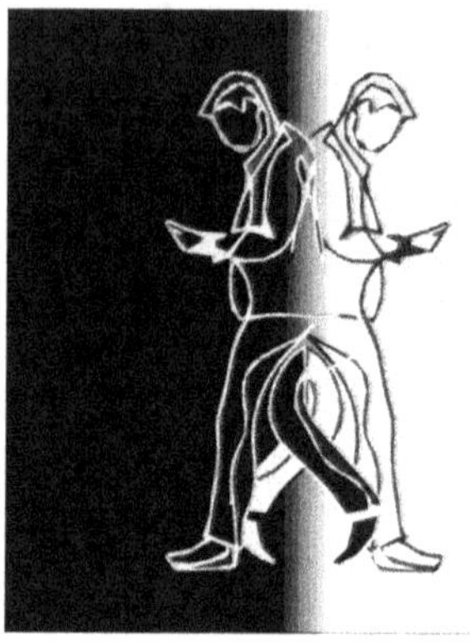

Drowsy eyes stared into the mirror,
A fagged-out animal gazed back,
Burdened under vows of the world,
Lost himself on the life-track.

Shading himself through the filter of society,
He let himself fade and droop,
Individuality long forgotten,
He struggled hard trying to fit in the groups.

Endless comparisons disquieted him,
Doubting his worth, he wrestled unease.
"What is life?" he tried to fathom,
As the mankind continued its ruthless tease.

Then came a relentless, hellish day,
He promised he would make himself rise,
Going inside his subconscious psyche,
To the imaginary problems, he waved some
goodbyes.

Now, shimmering eyes met the mirror,
His own essence stared back,
Awakened to his inner self,
He found his way back on track!

His Heart Skipped A Beat

Drenched in blood,
His skin felt cold,
Parched lips shivered,
His life – about to lose the hold.
Tears in his eyes mingled with the gore,
He clenched his fist as the guns on the field
roared.
Is this the end? His brain pounded in the
heat,
As his pupils enlarged, his heart skipped a
beat...

What had happened?
When did it blast?
In that troop in the fight,
Will he breathe his last?
Thoughts of his wife, made his teeth chatter
In the split of a second, he saw her heart
shatter.
Infuriated, he rose up – never to quit.
As he trembled on his legs, his heart skipped
a beat...

Whining of his newborn,
Echoed in his ears,
To let the tot grow strong,
He must forget his tears.
Looking up at the sky, he smiled at his
mother,
She blessed him with beam of light, now
nothing could bother.
Indignation pumped his blood, he took hold
of his kit,
As his fingers shivered on the gun, his heart
skipped a beat...

At the top of his lungs,
He yelled out a cry,
Blood-bathed flesh,
Tried to hold his head high.
Pulling the trigger, he stumbled in the run,
He made bullets rain, out of his creepy gun.
Abruptly on the ground he fell, acutely and
severely hit,
As he struggled to keep his eyes open, his
heart stopped the beat!!!

The Pencil

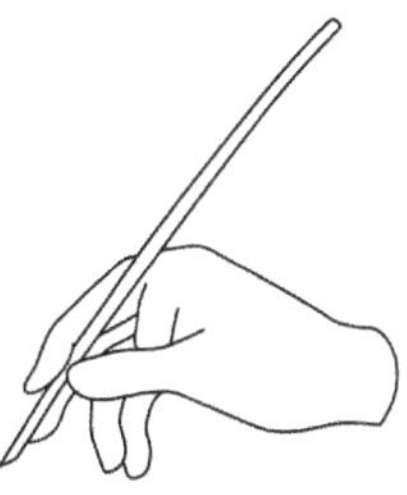

Stumbling through the pages, the pencil
began its cruise,
Breaking lead, laughing aloud, as she got two
friends in her blues...

The sharpener turned her short yet graceful
on the stride,
Having a friend like him has added sugar to
her pride.

The eraser wiped all the blunders she made,
The pencil chuckled as her mistakes got
slayed.

Both of them carved a lovely place in her
heart,
But she grew dependent on them for every
art.

One day, know not where eraser and
sharpener hide,
Only to make the pencil confident on her
ride...!

The Path

Through the narrow path,
Where sand and stones giggled at me,
I walked forward, stout-hearted,
Sipping a cup of toothsome tea.

Fiery rain poured over me,
Trying hard to muddle my grace,
To its disguise, it found me marching,
Unshrinking - with a smile on my face.

The other end of wrathful path
Held some light and shine,
No matter how darkness threatened,
With firm steps I chose- not to tremble and
whine.

Not afraid of the hitches on the path,
Which never saw a man so brave,
Piloting my spirit fearlessly,
I laid my troubles in a cozy grave!!

Sweat Your Skin

As the dawn arrives,
Get the hell up and give it a whirl,
Getting the work done, dig out your pearl
Put your body in action, with pain have some
fun,
Sweat your skin at dawn, then smirk at the
rising sun!

Let go of what you feel,
There is no time to cry or weep.
Days won't stop for you,
Sharpen your punches, let your victories reap.
Grind your bones heartily, to give your mind
a forward-run,
Sweat your skin during the day, then smirk at
the blazing sun!

To polish your elbow grease,
Show up on the field – inevitable
Life will fly swiftly,
Trying to knock you from the table.
Drudge your muscles warmly, get that
grueling shit done,
Sweat your skin at dusk, then smirk at the
setting sun!

Labor through the journey,
Do some exhausting back-breaking.
This is the real game, my friend,
Cease to think of your obstructive aching.
Exert yourself with the highest bounce of the
might,
Sun is far asleep, now sweat your skin
through the night!

The King

Amidst the whispers of leaves, the chirping of
birds,
The gushing of water, the growling of herds.
Bowed their heads the beasts, some raised the
horn,
In the woods in the middle of the jungle, a
cub was born.

Grabbed his heart the fear, when the rivals
stopped his way,
Unaware of majestic soul, he struggled to get
away,
Back to his den somehow, he managed to run,
Under the skin of father, he learnt how to get
it done.

Days passed, on him the yellow-gold coat did
shine,
Regal blood in his veins turned his mind
leonine.
Maned – in reddish brown, muscular had he
become.
Grew into Lion – courageous he stood –
shouldering what may come.

With commanding eyes and a mind untamed,
With menacing growls that left spines
maimed,
Bowed the heads of the beasts, some raised
the horn,
In the woods in middle of jungle, The King
was Born!!!

CHOICE

To be or not to be, is that truly the question?

Choice is the greatest powerhouse...
Which can awaken a lion out of a mouse...
Be calm, stay strong, walk unshaken...
Never regret the road which you haven't
taken...

Remember,
Filling your heart with happiness is the only
mission...
Then,
'To be or not to be' won't exist as a
question...!

ANGUISH

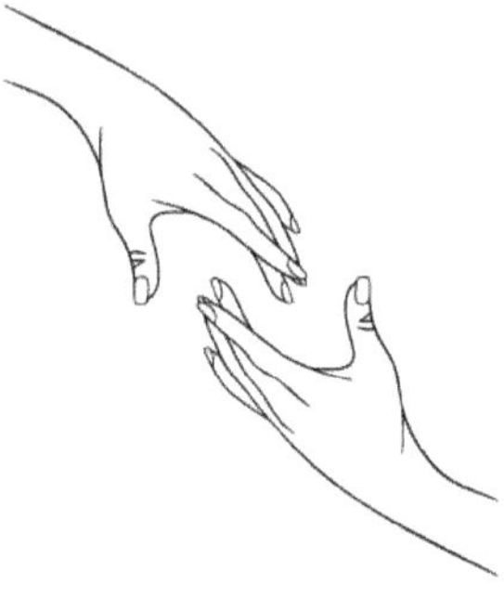

Don't forget how I arrived in your life, like a
knight with armor,
Then why pierce my heart, which earlier
seemed charmer?

Even today, through my veins, the current of
love flows,
Baby, sighting you walk away, my sorrowful
heart blows.

Back then, my heart was thumping a frantic
beat,
How on the earth could you hear, if your ears
are covered with intent of cheat.

I don't know why I let myself dive,
Only if I knew, you wouldn't hold me in high
tide.

Remember the days when we together had
juice of lime?
Now I wonder, was love merely a question of
time?

MISERY

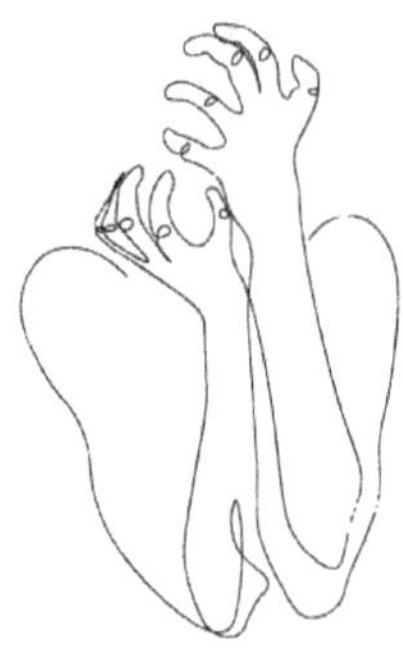

In the crisp, sunlit weather,
Our chemistry began to grow...
When the black clouds gathered
Why did you choose to go...?

Toxic are not
Just alcohol and drugs...
Poisonous were your
Fake kisses and hugs...!

I decided never again
To think of you in any way,
Yet, to my surprise,
My heart loves to disobey...

Just as rain follows the summer,
There is no doubt...
When the warmth disappears,
The heart needs to cry out...!!!

The God Is Talking To
Me

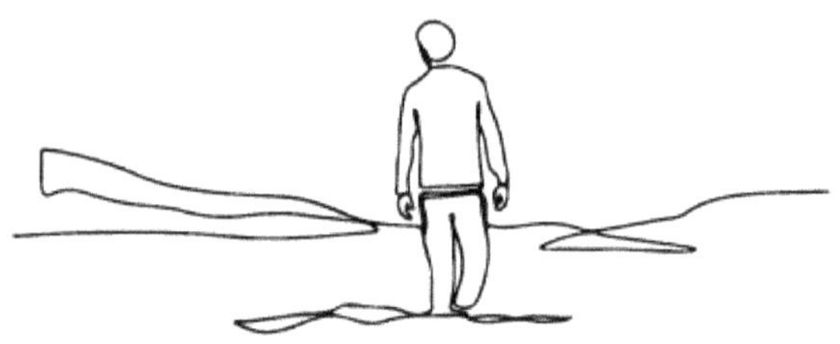

In the chilled, fresh, and awakening morning,
Through the soft kiss of the cold air, I feel...
Through the whispering movements of trees, I
see
Yes, God is speaking to me...

Through the clouds striding above my head,
Through the sun shining after my bed,
Through the beams of hope and optimism I
see,
Yes, God is speaking to me...

Though the ominous flashes lightening I see,
Through the gentle drizzle cascading on me,
Through the breezing waves of eternal sea—
Yes, God is speaking to me...

When I rise and fall and again – fall
My dreams diminish, seemed meaningless and
small.
Before I quit, roared the subconscious me,
That's when I found, God was speaking to
me!!!

Who Is God?

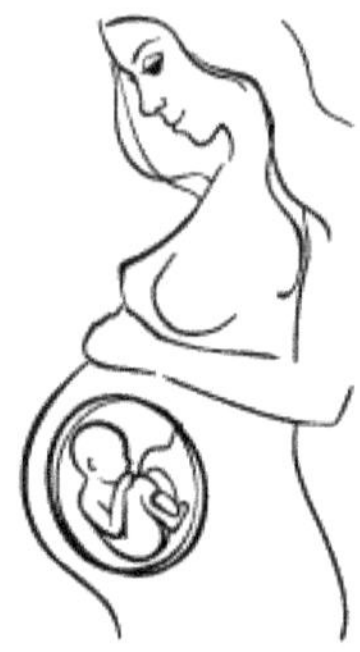

As a kid, for the first time I visited temple,
Folding hands in front of a stone, I found its importance ample.
Mom gestured me to close eyes and I gave a nod,
Wondered, standing over there – Who is God?

Watched devotional shows, read devotional stories,
With new story, I had new queries,
People call Him the Creator, people call Him a fraud,
Lost in thoughts, I asked – Who is God?

When I fell ill, her nights turned sleepless,
When I got hurt, her heart was restless.
She prays, says our hearts are connected with
him through a cord,
I asked her the only unanswered question –
Who is God?

The days passed but I hunted the answer of
mine,
I realized, she struggled with me till month
nine,
For me, as a kid, it sounded odd,
Then I found – WHO IS GOD...!!!

Chose Your Pain

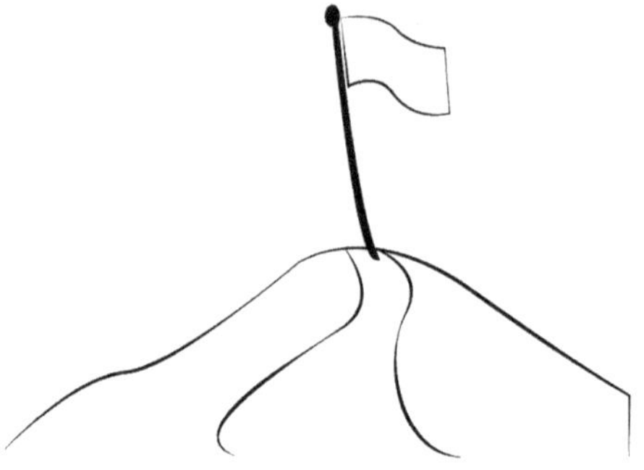

When your feelings control you,
The endgame has begun...
Seek the balance between the desires and
detachment,
That will make you intrepidly run...

Make yourself strong, so the spirit
Within you light the matches in your eyes...
And, let the world wonder from where did
those eternal sparkles arise...

Don't live your life in a way
That you'll regret before you die...
With excitingly thudding heart,
Live, breath, and fly.

Remember,

With mere positive thinking,
You can never gain...
To grow and bloom, you must
Choose your pain...!

Strings of My Heart

On a refreshing hour of daybreak,
On a cold dawn by the lake,
Come to me, Oh Darling, don't stand apart,
With zestful fingers of yours, play the strings
of my heart...

On a golden hour of the noon,
On a Spring's Day, when the flowers bloom,
Come to me, Oh Baby, lets make love into an
art,
With your pearly-diamond eyes, tease the
strings of my heart...

On a freezing hour of the sunset,
On a frosty eve of winter, hard to forget,
Head to me, Oh Love, of my life be a
dominant part
With the rosy arcs of yours, poke the strings
of my heart...

On an enthusiastically vibrant day,
When I want you to be here and stay,
Run your way down to me, Oh My
Sweetheart,
Giving all of you up to me, enjoy the strings
of my heart...!

NATURE HAS CRAVINGS

While the materialistic world penetrates your skin,

Keep in mind,

There is a wind, yearning to touch you...

There is the Sun, longing toy kiss you...

There is the Rain, craving to drizzle on you as if insane drug...
There is Nature, with open arms, thirsting for your hug...
***

MEANINGLESS FEELING

No one can understand what organisms are
we...
To what extent our heart feels, we can never
see...

What and why we feel, my heart wonders...
To seek the fake happiness our life wanders...

Happiness is something which we can never
find...
What we find is actually, forceful belief of our
mind...

Sadness is something which we can never feel...
What we feel is because our belief kneels...

***

SOUL OF WARRIOR

The sky gets cloudy; distress haunts your
brain,
That's the moment you don't shiver, like a
raging combatant you train.
Sitting idle, showing your back won't make
life easier,
Weave your way through fire, awaken the soul
of warrior.

Isolated are the extra miles – uncanny, eerie
and black,
That's the time you sweat your blood off the
beaten track.

No one's coming to back you up, you are your
savior,
To shed the blood on extra mile, awaken the
soul of warrior.

When self-doubt lingers in your head,
swallows your possibilities to be the best,
That's the point you don't allow it gobble, to
the doubt you bravely arrest.
With conviction walk focused, make your
moves strong and heavier,
Slay the doubt with your mighty sword,
awaken the soul of warrior.
On this noble conquest, procrastination
strides in, makes you standstill,
Don't let your blood reverse the flow, clasp in
your palm the Herculean will.
Before the time lets you bleed, place your feet
ahead – be the frontier,
Carrying off the crowns before time, awaken
the soul of warrior.

Distractions hijack your imaginations, in
fantasies you seem to play,
Shake your nerve to reality, throw the fancies
at the bay.
Dauntless you become, being hard you sow
the actions memorial,
Streaking through the obstructions, awaken
the soul of warrior.

As you conquer every step, arrogance may try
to amuse,
Be grounded Oh Fighter, to pomposity and
egotism you refuse.
Valiant is your heart, save it – be your own
courtier,
Wrecking arrogance in pieces, awaken the
soul of warrior.

You pass the ordeals, Comfort smiles at you -
locks you in its handcuffs,
Sneering at your eyes, to your honor and
discipline - it pleasantly puffs.

That's the moment you stood like a gallant
soldier in the face of all those barriers,
Look, your mind is unshackled, never let sleep
– The Soul of Warrior!
***

We Are the Sinners

Watch your head, O Mortal, show them not
disdainful Pride,
We are on a journey here, be humble on this
marvelous ride.
Don't feed arrogance to look scornfully down
at the beginner,
Befriending the Devil each day, O Mortal, we
are the sinners!

Watch your hunger, O Earthling, let it not
turn into Greed,
Hankering for fake materialism, don't you
crave to get mislead.

Rapacity quashes you, ruins your inmost
winner,
Hand in hand with the Evil, O Earthling, we
are the sinners!

Watch your instinct, O Man, bail yourself out
of Lust,
Save passion for right drive, not for
temporary thirst.
False desire cuts you, makes your thoughts
thinner,
Laughing aloud with Lucifer, O Man, we are
the sinners!

Watch your feelings, O Human, behold
without being Envious,
Triumphing over your emotions, breath the
air of genius.
Kick the discontent out, it makes you the
jealous grinner,
Smirking along with Satan, O Human, we are
the sinners!

Watch your gut, O Creature, let not eyes
sparkle for Gluttony,
Chewing and drinking with no control, fades
the sparkles in agony.
Wolfishness in eating dims your shine and
shimmer,
Burping intoxicated, O Creature, we are the
sinners!

Watch your anger, O Fleshy Bones, don't burn
in your Wrath,
Becoming furious in the desirous world
dwindles your math.
Indignant outrage drowns you even in the
calm rivers,
Raging like the Rebellion, O Fleshy Bones, we
are the sinners!

Watch your ventures, O Living Soul, why to
be an actionless sloth?
Laziness surging in the body turns you into a
sluggish loath,

Take that blow, take that action, make
yourself move for the greatness to shimmer,
Splitting the lucrative bond with The
Morning Star, let's stop being the Sinner!
***